I dedicate this book to my children, Maddie, Sammie and Connor.
My reason. My purpose. My loves.

And to my husband, Andrew,
for all your support, belief, love and loyalty.

And to my mum, Suzanne, the most dedicated mother.

BOUND
BOOKS

Published by Bound Books in 2023.
Bound Books is an imprint of Wildling Books Ltd.
Words © Gemma Douglas 2023. Illustrations © Craig Phillips 2023.

ISBN 978-1-99-117976-0 (paperback)
ISBN 978-1-99-117979-1 (POD)

www.wildlingbooks.com

STANDING ON THE EDGE OF

Motherhood

Gemma Douglas

The Motherhood Project

Introduction

I started The Motherhood Project (online blog through Facebook and Instagram – @themotherhoodprojectnz) back in 2017 as a way to help and guide myself through the life-altering journey I had started with my firstborn. I moved to a new city when my children were very young and I knew very few people. I was craving support and connection outside of the four walls I had found myself in for the majority of the time, and I found it online. It was a place I could talk honestly about the highs and lows and the anxiety and love that comes with birthing small humans into the world. What began as a way of expressing my experience grew into a community of mothers sharing experiences online.

It is now a community of over 200,000 around the world. I also now have a 'sister' project called The Conscious Project NZ (@theconsciousprojectnz) for my breathwork business for adults and kids.

The Motherhood Project has been like having many close friends who get where I am at. It has been the village that was missing in my early days of parenting. It has been a place where we have shared vulnerably and honestly, and in doing so have given each other the wings to fly.

I never set out to be a writer. What I offer in my writing is a raw and unfiltered insight into the mind of a mother – a true and often unorganised jumble of thoughts that traverse each day like a rollercoaster.

What I have noticed is the power of sharing my stories. This stream-of-consciousness writing has given so many other mothers permission to lay down their fears. It is this that has driven me to keep going with The Motherhood Project even when I've wanted to let it rest.

I hope that this collection is worthy of a place on your nightstand. As my own journey shifts and changes from being the mother of small children to being the mother of grown children, I decided it was time to close this chapter of my life with a curation of many of the thoughts and words that have got me through.

I thank you with my whole heart for being part of The Motherhood Project with me, without you I would have fallen more often. You lifted me up and made me feel seen. A deliberate decision was taken to curate this collection as is.

Instead of presenting it in coherent chapters or sections, it runs as a stream of consciousness.

It traverses and jumps from highs to lows, through joys and heartaches, just like motherhood itself.

There is no single trajectory that makes sense of the passing of time in motherhood; there is only the journeying of each day as it comes.

The only certainty we can have about our becoming a mother – that at one time or another we will all feel joy and pain.

As mothers, we come to surrender and embrace it all on our journeys, so that is what I have tried to present here in this collection.

This a real snippet of how motherhood swings between polarities, between calm and chaos.

My hope is that you find yourself in these words and, in doing so, find that you are not alone in your experience of motherhood.

Standing on the edge of motherhood

Here I am standing on the edge of motherhood
Unsure if I will fly or fall
And so, with bated breath, I step over the edge
From maiden to mother
And I fall
I fall
I fall
And just as I am about to hit the bottom
I grow wings
And begin to fly
Alongside all the mothers before me

Measuring motherhood

Try to measure your parenting on what it is you accomplished today instead of where you fell short:

Today my child was fed, comforted, cleaned and loved
I worked hard for my family today

I tried my best under challenging circumstances

Simple gestures

Our needs as mothers are no different from those of our babies.

We deserve to be surrounded and touched with love.

We deserve to be held up and cradled with support.

We deserve a shoulder to cry upon.

We deserve to hear that everything is going to be okay.

As a mother, it is these simple gestures that mean the world to us.

Underprepared

Raising my child as I still learn to grow up myself
is the most challenging thing I have ever done.

In nearly every new phase of motherhood, I've felt underprepared.

Yet somehow.

We have figured it out together
along the way.

My child has been my biggest teacher
and motherhood my greatest journey.

I never knew

Tears are never far from the surface in motherhood

Tears that come straight from the heart

often unstoppable.

Tears of joy
frustration
exhaustion
and pure love.

Through tears, motherhood has uncovered both

a fierceness
      and vulnerability
           within me
              I never knew existed.

Identity

I remember after having my first baby,
I said to a dear friend, 'I don't know who I am anymore.'
I felt my whole identity had been upended.
I felt the inevitable push and pull of this new life, motherhood, against the previous
version of me.
I suddenly craved that old life.
My whole identity went through a process of being reborn.
Of finding myself again.
Stronger and more beautiful.
A journey we will all go on as we move from maiden to mother.

Re-learning

I used to take life for granted at times.

Until I gave birth to a life I loved more than my own.

Since then, I am learning how important it is to look after myself.

Because I am everything to this little being.

Motherhood has scared me, taught me and awakened me.

Trying

This is for you, mama.
The one trying so hard right now.
Trying to do the right thing.
Trying to be the best mum you can be.
Trying to practise self-care.
Trying to stay open.
Trying to hold on to what is important and let go of what's not.
Trying to find your flow.
Trying to survive.
Trying to find the balance between being a woman and a mother.
Trying to stay in the present moment.
Trying to love yourself.
Trying to just be, among all the doing.

Let go of the trying for a moment.
You are doing enough.

Words

Words all mothers deserve to hear:

You still matter.
Struggling does not mean you are failing.
Your body does not need to bounce back.
Your mental, emotional and physical health matter more than ever.
No matter what age your child is, you will always encounter new challenges.
You deserve a break – without feeling guilty.
You are doing the best you can.

How can I support you?

The ideal

I wasn't ready for motherhood.

But I don't think anyone is.

I was ready for the ideal

which is very different from the real.

I learnt on the job, learning from my mistakes.

Growing into the strength required.

And digging to the depths necessary

to be the mum I need to be.

Fierce power

There is a fierce power that is unleashed when a woman becomes a mother.
Full of potential and motivation to become the best of herself for her child.
We often forget this power as we juggle all the balls that motherhood hands to us.
So gently place each one down.
Then carefully choose the ones you will pick back up.
And honour these.
Remember to breathe.
Remember your power.
For you are simply becoming.

GENTLE POSTPARTUM REMINDERS 1

• Postpartum is equal parts hard and beautiful.

• If you have birth trauma and conflicting feelings around your birth – talk about them.

• Matrescence is a term used to describe the identity shift you go through when you become a mother (like teenagers and adolescence).

• It is worth seeing a pelvic floor health physio six to 12 weeks after you've given birth.

• Cluster feeding is when your baby feeds a lot through the night to help bring in your milk. This usually happens on day two or three and it can be really challenging so soon after birth.

Remembering

Which memories will you recall, little one?

Will you remember when I raised my voice as you climbed the gate?
Or will you remember that I cuddled you to sleep?

Will you remember that I cried today?
Or will you remember that we belly-laughed instead?

Perhaps you won't remember much, but these years are shaping you as a person.
This excites and terrifies me all at once.

I long to know how I can help you remember me as a better mama, a wiser mama.

And so, I will just keep trying from one moment to the next, hoping that is what you will
remember.

Friend

Sometimes all you need is that one friend
The one you text in the middle of the night
The one with whom you can share the pressures and expectations of motherhood
uncensored
Then chat together about how none of that matters
That friend who convinces you through your tears that you are doing an amazing job
The one who will never judge, shame or offer advice when all you want is an ear
Whether you are pregnant, have little ones or teenagers all you need is that one friend
The one who is gold
Pure gold

Husband

We are both tired.
Tired from keeping the small versions of ourselves alive.

So, our love right now is made up of small gestures:

Writing erotic notes on the shared supermarket list, knowing it will make you smile as you check it off.

Putting on my favourite song in the bathroom while I have a shower.

Getting out of bed with our early-rising toddler and pulling the door shut so that I can have just a little more sleep.

Asking each other if we want comfort or solutions when things get challenging and we wrap our arms around one another.

Some days it's me and some days it's him who contributes more.
It isn't always 50/50, some days it looks more like 70/30 as we help each other to get through.

Love now is the little moments of acknowledgement, the letting you know they are thinking of you.

At the moment we have no time or energy for grand gestures, but that's okay.
Even if one of us did, the other would probably be too tired to do it anyway.

Mental load

As a mother your mental load is heavy.
You think not only for yourself but for every member of your family.
Not simply what they need to eat or drink or when they need to sleep.
You are also thinking of everyone's emotional, physical and mental well-being.

It is then no wonder that thinking about your own schedule and well-being can seem overwhelming.

Another person to worry about.

You, mother, are at capacity.

Don't throw guilt on top when things don't quite go to plan.

You are doing the best you can.

Right now

Slow down, mama.
Lay down that mental load
heavy with expectations handed to you by society.
Lay down your arms
heavy from carrying others.

As capable and powerful as you are
all hearts need nourishment, peace and stillness including yours.

Try to fill your heart
see the sun rising and falling
try not to see the to-do lists.

Fill your heart with the laughter and smiles of your children and lover, not the worries
and what-ifs.

Try not to miss the moments between the tick boxes.
Don't miss the magic among the chaos and clutter.

You are missing you.
And the world is missing you too.

So, just for a moment, opt out of the race with no destination.

Right now is waiting for you to arrive.

GENTLE REMINDERS

• Let the tears flow. Crying lowers cortisol (the stress hormone) and soothes your nervous system.

• Guilt has no place around how you feed your baby.

• Trust your gut, your intuition. If something doesn't sit right with you concerning your child, listen to it and talk to someone.

• You are the expert on your child. No one else.

• You may miss your old life more than you thought. It's okay to grieve.

I hope you know

When my presence was distant and heavy

and my patience was failing

followed quickly by apologies and cuddles

It wasn't you my love

It was my battle not yours

My love and devotion to you never wavered

But I had to learn to love myself

through all the versions of me I met along the way

when all I craved was to show you my best

I'm sorry I didn't handle the tiredness sometimes

that my words were short and flat

that it created a shadow over my mood

and dimmed the light in my eyes sometimes

I hope you know

I tried my best with the tools I had at the time

That your light sparked my own time and time again

That I always found a way to get back up

That our simple days were more than enough

I know now we weren't missing anything

because our world had all we needed

because I was your everything

and you are my forever

I just really hope you know

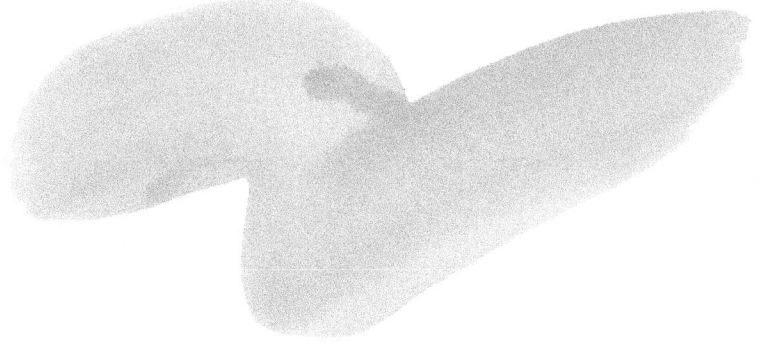

All that matters

Affirmation

I am listening to my heart and trusting my intuition.

I am the perfect mother for my child.

Society does not need to grant me permission to choose how to raise my child.

Nor does it deserve to.

All that matters is that it comes from a place of love.

Of this, I am already sure.

Rearranged

Motherhood pulled me apart piece by piece
and rearranged me entirely.
I cry more.
I laugh more and I ache more.
Through these postpartum years, at times, I have felt like a completely different person.
It is only now that I am slowly piecing myself back together again.
With newfound love and respect for myself and all mothers.
As I become the person I am meant to be.

Put it down

I ask you, mama, for a moment to release the heaviness from your shoulders.

Put down
the should
and
pressures you feel.

Place one hand on your heart and tell yourself:

I am doing my best with the knowledge and tools I have.

Beautiful mother

In case you need reminding,

You are a beautiful mother.

Your smile lights up your child's face.

You are more than enough.

You are doing an amazing job.

You are a mother, a woman and a friend.

You are a multitasking superhero.

Perspective

When I wake up, I get to hug my child.

Drink clean water.

Breathe in fresh air.

Take a shower.

Feel safe in my home.

Eat a nutritious breakfast.

Move my body.

Perspective is everything.

Sending love to those whose world has been turned upside down.

SELF-CARE MORNING ROUTINE FOR BUSY PARENTS

1. Wake up and try not to look at your phone (until at least after step 7).

2. With your eyes closed, complete a one-minute scan of your entire body. Notice any tension and inhale deeply into that area.

3. Put on your dressing gown.

4. Go to a window or walk outside (whatever the weather). Take three deep breaths, emptying the stale air from your lungs. In through your nose and out through your mouth with a loud sigh. Take a child with you if you need.

5. Name five unique things you are grateful for right now.

6. Create a positive affirmation for the day. For example: 'I have everything I need to make today a great day.'

7. Prepare a nutritious breakfast – something you look forward to eating.

8. If needed – inhale for four, hold for four, exhale for four, hold for four. Do this 10 times.

Telling myself

I've started telling myself I'm a good mum.

I didn't for years because I was so exhausted and worried.
I felt guilty for not enjoying every moment.

Yet, those were the times I needed to hear it most.

I have come to realise that even when I struggle, I am still a good mum.

Because in every moment I am trying my best

And sometimes I just need to be reminded of that.

Motherhood isn't glamorous

Motherhood isn't glamorous.
Sometimes it's walking into the bathroom to see toothpaste smeared everywhere.
Followed by looking in the mirror to see my mascara smeared under my eyes.
It's walking out of the bathroom and knowing I will clean it tomorrow.
It is being too tired to shower when I know I really should.

Sometimes I just sit with my kids in the darkness so they go to sleep faster, without
singing songs, reading books or talking about our day. Sometimes I just kiss them good
night and tell them it's time to sleep.

Sometimes I have the energy to do it all, the lullabies and the evening chats,
and sometimes I don't.

Motherhood is full of ups and downs, intensities and calm, challenges and beauty.

Motherhood isn't glamorous, nor is it meant to be.

It is there for learning
For falling down
and getting back up again.

It isn't glamorous but it is worth embracing and cherishing.

A new kind of society

Instead of society celebrating competition, status and individual success.

Instead of society measuring productivity in metrics.

Imagine if we celebrated mothers looking after themselves.

Celebrated mothers asking for help and practising self-care.

No part of motherhood can ever be measured in metrics.

Motherhood is not a competition, nor a status, nor can it ever be successful alone.

It is time for a new kind of society,
one that cherishes the mother the way she deserves.

All in time

As a mother, you might feel you aren't valued or appreciated much right now, and your life may look so different to what it was before.

You may feel like you don't have any life outside of your family or your four walls.

We all feel like this at times. Your friends have felt it too.

This little person of yours values appreciates and regards you as the most important thing in their entire world right now.
They just don't show us in ways we are used to.

But if we watch, they will show us in the most beautiful of ways:

The look in their eye when they gaze at you,
the touch of their hand when they reach for you,
the way you and only you are the one they call to comfort them.

It is in the way they feel safe enough to show you all their emotions – because you are their safe place.
It's how they fall asleep the fastest upon you because they instinctively remember being part of you.

You will one day reconnect with your friends and have space to make new ones.
You and your partner will have time to connect again. You will one day have your own space and you will grow, love and blossom into your new self.

All in time– this I promise, and you will owe this beautiful transformation to them.

Ripple effect

There is a ripple effect when mothers start caring for themselves properly.

When they do their own soul-searching and deep work.

It transforms not only their own lives.

But their children too.

Make the time.

Still you

Dear postpartum mama,

Life right now might be more challenging than you ever thought it would be.

You may not recognise parts of yourself – your body, mind or identity.

But you are still you.

The other parts are there wrapped up safe.

When you are feeling stronger, unwrap yourself a little, remember those other pieces.

Bit by bit, you will come to recognise yourself again.

This phase of your life has been devoted entirely to another.

Breathe it in. Be kind to yourself.

This phase, like all others, will pass.

You. Are. Enough.

She is exhausted
But she keeps going because there is simply no choice
No one can see how truly exhausted she is
How her bones ache from holding everyone up
How her mind is overflowing from overthinking
But it is not her body or mind that keeps her going
It is love
The love that touches her soul
The love that keeps her giving and giving
The love she hopes will be enough
She hopes she will be enough
And she is
You. Are. Enough.

Juxtapositions

The life I knew before is gone.
In its place is something gloriously chaotic and beautifully exhausting.
My life now is filled with overwhelming love and purpose that brings me to my knees.
A love that can pick me up again in an instant.
A love set deeply into my child's eyes.
So, the only thing I have to do is to look at their face, and I am lifted into the glorious and the beautiful.

Sometimes

Sometimes as a mum I choose tough love over giving in.
Sometimes instead of discipline, I choose to hold them and give them a long hug.
Sometimes I turn on the TV so I can sit or make dinner.
Sometimes I let my child sleep on me all day or night.
Sometimes I choose not to give in, in the hope of a lesson learned.

The reason for these decisions is of no concern to others. Everyday choices that seem small to others are huge to us.
It is a constant battle of good or bad, right or wrong.

There is no training, no manual, no study or exam to graduate as a mum.

I worry constantly about how I am shaping my children, and what ideas, beliefs, thoughts and values I am teaching them.
I worry about which things to hide from them in the hope they don't make the same mistakes as I did.

I worry about what they pick up on subconsciously as I live as this imperfect human when the only thing I want to be for them is perfect.

Decisions

Every day we make decisions based on what is in front of us at that moment.
We use a mixture of common sense, intuition, instinct and the best of our intentions
to guide us.

But when we inevitably get it wrong, we are given a lesson to learn
and that is okay.
When we do choose right, it is a moment to celebrate

But one thing remains, we always try our best and when we know better,
we can do better.

A mother's heart

The love a mother feels for her child is different from any other type of love.

It need not be reciprocated and comes from an endless well.

A well that is nurtured by Mother Nature herself.

It fills not only a mother's heart but every fibre and cell of her being.

People will talk

Mama, people will talk no matter what you do.

They will agree or disagree, shame or accept.

They will judge you if you work and judge you if you don't.

Some with the best of intentions and others not so.

At the end of each day, yours is the voice that matters most.

That feeling in the pit of your stomach.
The feelings you feel when the world around you finally quietens and you tune into your heart.

So let them talk, advise, judge and suggest.

Just know that, at the end of the day, it is what is in your heart that is best.

The mess can wait

Mess surrounds me
My eyes dart to the dishes
The washing pile
The bread you tried to butter smeared across the bench
The overflowing rubbish
And then my eyes fall on you
Your eyes have been staring at me the whole time, watching my every move
Wondering when my eyes will fall upon you
Looking at me as though I am the most important thing in the world
But I know as soon as I look at you it is all over
I remember that you are the most important work and the rest is the distraction
I admit that some days I get this the wrong way around

So, thanks for the reminder, kid

Right now, the mess can wait

Reparenting

I can't be the mother I want to be
If I am not the woman
I need to be for myself

WHEN YOU'RE FEELING TIRED

How to cope with sleep deprivation as a parent:

Legs up the wall

Drink loads of water

Breathwork (in for four, hold for four, out for four, hold for four)

Take a one-minute cold shower

Listen to a yoga nidra

Play 'doctors'. Your child is the doctor and you are the patient who needs to lie down

Choose an easy dinner – perhaps a platter or a takeaway

Replace guilt with self-compassion

Find some sunshine and lie in it

Get outside

Walk in nature

We all feel it too

To you, mama,
having a rough day.
To you who can't bear the mess, but can't face cleaning it up.
To you who can't wait to go to bed but knows you will be up through the night.
To you who daydreams of a life gone by, while simultaneously feeling guilt for
this longing.
Yet, you are also grateful.

What you are feeling is okay. We feel it too.
One day, your house will be clean again and you will sleep again.
As you grow into this new self, I promise that one day you will look back with proud eyes
and a full heart at your journey and transformation.

Like that

Please, mama
The way your child loves you, love yourself like that.

The way your child forgives you, forgive yourself like that.

The way you nourish your child, nourish yourself like that.

The way you hold your child, hold yourself like that.

Don't wait until you are better, do it now as you are.

Your child will then follow in your footsteps, watching and learning how to love themselves without condition.

Weak is strong

Mama,
Being strong
Also means
Being able to tell people
When you are feeling weak.

That is a next-level type of strong.

You are their home

Mama,
your little one adores you.
You are their home.
You are their safe place.
You are their world.
None of us knows what we are doing.
But we are all doing the best we can.
Keep living from your heart.
Because your little one adores you.

The gifts they give

My children make me:
Laugh
Cry
Play
Dance
Question myself
and seek the truth

All the things that truly matter and all the things that make me vulnerable.

Crying therapy

Mama, when was the last time you cried?
The beauty of shedding tears is you are clearing the pain of past memories.
You are releasing fear from your body, leaving a path of peace.
Crying is a way to heal.
Tears are not a weakness, they are surrender, vulnerability and cleansing.
To cry is to release, to cleanse. It is a form of self-love and strength towards yourself.

Honour the feelings you feel and hold all of yourself in the same unconditional love that you hold your children.

Doubtful

Motherhood can cloud us in doubt about who we are.
We come to realise that so much of what we used to worry about no longer matters.
Yet, at the same time, we have no idea what we are doing.

But there lies the secret. We begin to realise that none of us knows what we are doing –
and that it is okay.

As mothers, we are called to show up just as we are.
We are pulled apart piece by piece and put back together again, more courageous and
more beautiful than ever before.
With scars to show for the journey.

You won't show up perfectly every time, so don't beat yourself up with negative self-talk.
You are doing your best at this moment.

Breathe deeply and know that you are enough.

Between worlds

In a moment, everything becomes foreign.
We are caught between our former self and this new terrified,
exhausted yet awakened self.
Knowing this is the start of something divinely beautiful.

Motherhood.

The soul that was within us for the past nine months has,
in a single moment, taught us the meaning of love beyond
words, beyond comparison, beyond life itself.

We are in a slow process of rebirthing.

When a baby is born so too is a mother, yet our transformation is not
yet complete.
The transformation takes time until we fully surrender to this new path.

This transformation begins slowly and unassumingly, pulling us
apart piece by piece, rearranging us entirely. Moulding, moving
and transforming our bodies and minds in a way that can never
be undone, nor would we want it to be.

Once this transformation is finally complete, our memories
of this rebirthing become distant.
We find it hard to imagine or remember who it was we
were before this.

Our former self becomes an old friend we once knew.
We are grateful for her yet we have grown apart.

A gift

My daughter,
You gave me a gift last night.
As I found myself sitting on my phone far away from the present moment.
You came to me in the darkness, long after you should have been sleeping.
Just needing me.
So I sat down on your bed and you grabbed my hand.
And unaware (or maybe so fully aware) you placed my hand upon your heart.
Your beautiful, soft, beating heart.
And in an instant I was there with you, all of me present.
As you fell asleep with my hand upon your heart, you left me contemplating the gift you had just given me.
The present moment.
Our present moment.
A reminder that life is best lived one single heartbeat at a time.

With you

When the heaviness of the day hits you.
When you wake and you know that it may get harder as the day goes on.
Know that we are carrying it with you.

When night comes and you find yourself standing more than lying.
When your eyes are open more than closed.
Know that we are standing with you.

When your body aches from moving and you want desperately to rest.
When there is no diagnosis beyond extreme lack of sleep.
Know that we are aching with you.

When tears start falling with questions left unanswered.
When the pressure needs releasing so you can find your strength again.
Know that we are crying with you.

When the only answer you can find is to simplify life more.
When the only thing left to do is cuddle more, bake more and play more.
Know that we are simplifying with you.

When you know deep in your bones this challenge of motherhood is the
most rewarding.
When you feel so much privilege and joy.
Know we are feeling this with you.

We are mothers.
Alone.
But in this together.

The fourth trimester + 1

She knew of the fourth trimester, those first three months after a baby is born.
The one meant for mother and baby to bond, to rest, to heal and to surrender.

She was told not to rush, not to return to the busy just yet.
She wanted desperately to embrace this time.

But
This wasn't her first baby; she already had another one too.
A child who was desperately struggling with this new little being suddenly taking
up all the space and time and energy that was once all hers.

She so desperately wanted someone to take her baby, to be with her firstborn,
to hold her and tell her everything was going to be okay.
Because, deep down, she needed to reassure herself of that too.

So, she did the best she could.

She asked for help, she cried and she felt like a failure at times, but she always
got back up again. She realised she wasn't failing.
She was learning to find her feet.
Alongside her first born, she was learning to dance again, finding their groove
and new normal together.

There were times of thriving but there were also times of surviving. And
moments she wished would stand still.

As time passed, she realised she was brave and she was capable.

She had done her very best.
She didn't get it all right, but in the same breath, she didn't get it all wrong either.

She had again stood in the fire of motherhood. Courageous and beautiful.

Piecing it back together

You
Courageous mama
Have been through so much.
And even in the depths of your biggest challenges, you find a way to carry on.
You are slowly uncovering a power and inner strength you never knew existed.
An inner strength that burns deep for your child and yourself.

Life has tried to break you, but you survived and you rise.

You are a mother.

Slowly you piece yourself back together again like a puzzle constantly evolving.

Your child the final piece that makes you whole.

Loving herself

One of the most beautiful things a mother can do for her family is to love herself deeply
Love herself so compassionately and unconditionally
Not waiting for a moment when she is better at anything, but right now
Just as she is
Just as you are
Love yourself as your child loves you
Forgive yourself as your child forgives you
And from that, they will grow to love themselves too

Your way

Mama
Here is your reminder.

Be unapologetically you.

Mother your way.
Work your way
and
Rest your way.

And while we are here, dress, play, eat and love in whatever way speaks your truth.

Forget the guilt and expectations to be someone other than you.

Your child wants nothing more than for you to be you.

Foundations

Mothers are the foundation.
The rock.
The glue.
The cement.
Holding their families together.
Holding society together.

Looking after a mother's health and well-being is vital for society.

Looking after a mother should not be some sort of unwarranted self-indulgence, but something they should feel empowered by.

It is not good enough anymore that mothers are simply surviving.

GENTLE POSTPARTUM REMINDERS 2

• Be incredibly kind to yourself with your thoughts. Lower your expectations... then lower them some more.

• Your body feels so foreign right now. It's sore, swollen, big and lumpy. It's also just grown a baby and birthed it. It needs a whole lot of love, not judgement.

• Leave room for great days and not-so-great days. The sleep deprivation can be all-consuming. Remember to breathe, lower your shoulders and release the tension.

• It's not just your baby growing, you are too. That means you need good food, sunlight, water and support.

• Skin-to-skin contact not only calms your baby, but will calm you too.

• Accept help, ask for help and don't try to be the perfect mum.

I see you

I see you at the café, in the car park, at the doctor's office.
I see you changing your little one in the car when the nappy exploded.
I see you trying to calm your toddler when they don't want to leave or share, and you see a meltdown about to unfold.
I see you attempting to cross the road with one child trying to do a runner while you're desperately trying to hold on to the pram containing the other.
I see you giving everything you've got trying to keep everyone happy.
I see you feeling as though you are just holding onto your sanity.
I see how intensely you are loving them, how you'd do anything for them.

You are amazing and irreplaceable

Sometimes we make eye contact and one of us gives a reassuring smile. These small gestures let us know we are seen.

So, if you see another mother today, please smile or ask them how they are. You never know what it might mean to her.
It is relationships and connections that can be a life-jacket keeping our heads above the tide of motherhood water.

The full story

She may seem like she has everything under control.
She may seem like she is put together.
She may make multi-tasking look like a breeze.
She may seem like such an optimistic person.
She may seem like she is organised.
She may seem like she handles it.
She may seem like she is perfect.

But she's not, she's really not.
Perfect is not possible for her or anyone else.

It's not that she is being fake, inauthentic or trying to hide behind a façade.

She just doesn't like to talk about it.
She is a private person who wants to focus on the positive and process the negatives in her own way.

She too cries and yells and feels guilt.
She judges herself and hurts just like everyone else.
She just closes the door first because that is where she feels safe.

We are all imperfect mothers, striving to be perfect for our children.
We all have different ways of expressing ourselves as we did before becoming mothers.

We don't know the details of everyone's journeys and we all entered this hood at different times and stages in our lives.

So let's not compare someone's middle to our beginning.

Or let's not compare at all

Because we can never know the full story

So let's support her anyway.

Investing in you

Mama,
you are worth investing in right now.
Burn your best candles.
Spray your favourite perfume.
Eat your favourite food and use your finest glasses.
For when you do, you will set off a ripple.
These small things bring you joy.
Your family will feel it too.
Don't wait for the perfect moment.
Cherish yourself now.

Finding me

Becoming a mother has become a period of intense evaluation of every part of my life.

Who I was.
Who I wanted to be.
My relationships.
My boundaries or lack thereof.
How I care for and loved myself.

It stirred up every mental, emotional, spiritual and physical cell in my body.
It left me with more purpose than I ever imagined.

Motherhood made me feel so completely out of my depth yet completely myself all at the same time.

Over

Sometimes you'll overstretch.
You'll overreach and give too much.
Your overthinking will devour every moment and your worry will grip you.
You will doubt yourself as your mind overflows with the deciding and the undeciding and the deciding again.

Find the gap between your thoughts, embrace the lull and silence that feel perhaps foreign.

Stop yourself from filling it – no noise, no jobs, no should be.
Let your shoulders fall and your jaw relax.
Fill that void with you – just you.

Ask yourself what it is you need.
What do you desire and crave right now?

Water, nourishing food, silence, laughter, peace, stillness, music, touch or sunshine?

Go find it. You are worthy and deserving of what you need.

Fill the void with self-love that overflows and has you ready to give again.

Breathe

My far away friend

Because we live far away and it's been so long, it doesn't mean I love you any less. I miss sharing things with you – wardrobes, secrets and meals. We went from best friends to weddings to mothers in what felt like such a short time. From seeing you daily, then weekly then yearly, to commenting on each other's posts. But when a chance meeting appears, it's like nothing has changed all these years. Perhaps the beverage has changed and the little loves that come along in our arms. I guess all I wanted to say is I miss you and me. I just needed to tell you that you are still in my heart after all these years.

Phases

Parenthood is made up of phases.
Empowering ones.
Debilitating ones.
Intense, gentle and hard ones.

Ones that will break us down and others that will build us up.

We are still allowed to find joy in parenthood and be grateful for the privilege while also struggling and finding it challenging.

We are allowed to break and crack a little – it's how the light gets in.

Helpers

So many mothers, when they need support,
don't reach out because they
don't want to be a nuisance to others.
But stop and think for a moment.
If another mother asked you for help,
you know you would gladly help her,
because it also feels good to be a helper.
Let others be helpers too.

Rituals in the dark

Sitting with my child while they fall asleep is a ritual in our house.
Yet I admit that some days it feels more like a bad habit than a ritual.
But deep down I know there is nothing bad about this habit.
It is simply what they need right now.
And this need will not be there forever.
Ritual or habit I will continue to sit with my child.
Until they no longer need me this way anymore.

For you

This one is for you.
The one who feels drained from the negative thoughts and feelings you never thought you'd have around motherhood.
The one who feels like the road out is too long with no end in sight.
The one who is so tired you struggle to string a sentence together let alone cook a meal or have a shower.
The one whose nights are spent up and down, lying on your child's floor dreaming of the nights you will once again sleep in your own bed, uninterrupted.
The one who is trying so hard to make the most of these 'magical' motherhood days everyone keeps talking about, yet all you feel is mundane.

You are not alone in these thoughts and, as clichéd as it sounds, it does get better.

Negative thoughts will still come, but you will get stronger and engage with them less.
One phase will pass into another and there will be ones you never want to end.
Your child will eventually sleep, even through the night, but the touch of your hand on their back will remain with them forever.
You will experience the magic among the mundane. The moments of pure gold will become more and more.
You will feel it and believe it when they say it's all worth it.

Let yourself cry in the bad moments and celebrate the great.

Whether you are surviving or thriving, every bit of this journey is important – just know that you are not alone.

GENTLE POSTPARTUM REMINDERS 3

• Read up about the fourth trimester. This will help you so much with your recovery, expectations and healing.

• Call your mum, sisters and best friends as often as you need, to laugh and cry with them.

• Get outside with the pram or front pack — fresh air and nature are amazing.

• You may miss the old you. You may feel bad for missing the freedom you used to have. This is so normal. You don't need to embrace the new you all at once. The other parts of you are safe in a box.

• Not everyone bonds with their baby straight away. Sometimes it takes time, hang in there.

• You may have a feeling of 'baby blues' — mood swings, irritability, sadness (caused by oestrogen and progesterone levels dropping). Generally, this resolves after a week or two. If it doesn't, talk to someone.

Still my baby

My baby, you are still my baby.
I promise.
Even though in a single moment everything looks different.
You look so much older and feel so much heavier.
I wish someone would come to hold your new sister.
Just so I can hold you.
Just so I can tell you everything is going to be okay.
Because I need to hear it too.
There will be hard days, I know.
I will crave your forgiveness on the days I do not get it right.
Those days I expect more from you than you are capable of giving.
Each day I will prove to you that, even though there are now two, my love will never
be halved.
And even though our time together is less right now,I still need you just as much as you
need me.

You just know

Mama, it all matters.
You know what their favourite food, snacks and ice cream are.
You know how they like their veggies and fruit cut and you make sure one doesn't touch the other on the plate.
You can tell when they are grumpy and just need a cuddle.
You know their favourite outfit, the position they sleep in at night and how many blankets they prefer.
You know the night light they like to have on, their favourite book and song.
You know their friends' names, what they are struggling with and what they are excited about.

You know of these even though they change daily.

So, at the end of a long day when you think to yourself – what did I do today?

I watched,
I listened,
I played,
I planned,
I loved,
I organised.

I created a home where my children feel safe, known and loved.

There is nothing more beautiful or important than that.

Yet

As mothers, we are mentally pushed beyond our perceived limit of exhaustion.
Yet we keep going.

We are emotionally pushed beyond our perceived limit of how much love our hearts
can hold.
Yet we love even more.

We are pushed physically beyond our perceived limit of pressure, pain and,
sometimes, trauma.
Yet we would take more of it if it meant we could hold our baby in our arms.

A dear friend

Some days we have to dig deep.
And we forget.
Perhaps you have forgotten to remind yourself lately just how powerful you really are.
Just how valuable growing and nurturing another soul really is.
Invite yourself to believe in you.
You are powerful.
You are strong.
You are more than enough.
This is the most important work.
Holding their hearts,
growing their bodies.
Your cells create their cells.
Take a deep breath and believe it when I say:
You are powerful even when you fall.
You are worthy just because.
You are strong because you get back up again.
Mama, treat yourself as you would a dear friend
with the love you so truly deserve.

My mother

I remember idolising my mum as I grew up.
She could do no wrong.

When I was old enough to realise she too was human, I still idolised her for what she did
for us.

I remember her working full-time and being tired.
But I also remember her stroking my forehead and the song she sang.
I remember the cuddles every time I couldn't sleep and the way she was always there
to talk.

I forget sometimes that, as I try to be the perfect mother, all my child needs is
connection, love and to feel heard.

Society

When mothers are at breaking point and told they just need more self-care.

There is a step missing.

What mothers need is community care and once they have that, there is space for self-care.

Different version of me

I try so hard to be a gentle parent.

But I'm not one all of the time.

Sometimes I am the impatient parent, the reactive parent and the struggling parent.

Sometimes I am the anxious parent, the exhausted parent and the overwhelmed parent.

But I am always the committed parent, the loving parent and the forever-trying parent.

You are the world

Mama, in the quiet of the night when all you can hear is your two hearts beating.

No matter what age your child is, you are exactly where you are meant to be.

You are the only one in the world they want.

You are the epitome of love and sacrifice.

You are a mother like all others.

And those mothers are all there with you.

It's the other things

Sometimes it's not parenthood that makes life challenging.

Sometimes being a parent is the only thing that keeps you going when life gets tough.

My season

This is my season.

My season of giving – my body, my nights, my time, my tears, my sleep.

My season of extremes – my love, my exhaustion, my vulnerability, my fears, my overwhelm, my happiness.

My season of change – my resisting, my transforming, my growing.

It is also my season of receiving.

You, my child.
My name – mama.
My purpose and path.
Your presence, perspective and trust.

So, when I feel over my head in this season of giving, extremes and change, I remember that even though I have given you everything right now.

This is just our season together.

The hardest part of mothering

I'm beginning to realise the toughest season of mothering you is yet to come.

The one where you create a story without me in it and make mistakes without me fixing them.

It is heart-wrenching yet soul-giving and I feel it happening minutely already.

This is my journey of letting go.

A day in the life of a mother

I'll be there in a minute.
Go put your shoes on.
Please check on your sister.
Go get a jersey on.
I'm going to count to three.
Go and get your brother, please.
I want you to sort it out yourselves.
I said go and put your shoes on.
Get in the car.
Go and put more clothes on.
You can have a piece of fruit.
Last time – put your shoes on.
I'm not going to ask you again.
Have a glass of water.
Eat what you are given.
Bring your dishes here.
Are you forgetting something?
It's bedtime.
Come and have a cuddle.
Go and brush your teeth.
Go to sleep.
Mummy is tired.
Come here.
I love you.
I'm sorry.
You are my world.

Doing it all

I know you're trying so hard right now.

Trying to be the conscious and responsive parent.
Trying to practise your own self-care.
Trying to hold onto friendships.
Trying to keep the house tidy.
Trying to keep the meals as healthy as you can.
Trying to love yourself.
Trying to find balance as a woman and a parent.
Trying to stay present.
Trying to survive.

You are trying so hard and sometimes it feels heavy.
So for a moment
Stop and breathe
Lower your shoulders and release the jaw
Let it go for now, and just be.

You are doing better than you think.

It is always enough

As I walk out of my child's room with my final good night
I noticed a familiar thought – Was I enough today?

Was I present enough?
Did I feed them well enough?
Was I on my phone too much?
Did I let them express themselves enough?
Enough Enough Enough.

Because sometimes I did do enough.
Other times I could have been better.

So, I thank the universe for another day to learn, to fall and to get back up again.

By example

My child won't do what I tell them to do, they will *be* who I am being.
If I always put myself last, my needs and my happiness.
If I always wear exhaustion like a badge of honour.
If I always feed myself last.
If I use words like 'I never get to'.
If I wait until I am burned out to rest.
If I allow people to cross my boundaries.
If I only speak of worries and eternal busyness.

I am not being who I desire them to be.

If I want them to find their joy
then I must search for and celebrate my own.
If I want them to feel contentment and peace
then I must show them how it feels.
If I want them to be a person who prioritises self-love, care and esteem
then it is me who must be the one I desire them to be.
Because they will be who I am being.
Not what I am doing.

Weaving worlds with words

As a parent, I automatically go to the worst-case scenario and then do everything in my power to rule it out.

So my child can fall asleep soundly, I create different worlds with my words. Reassuring them of their safety so that they can fall asleep soundly.

And I lie there next to them trying to solve the problems of the world as they sleep.

I realise,
it doesn't matter their age,
we all go through this in waves.

Alone, yet together. An army of forever-trying parents.
And there is great comfort in that.

All in one day

In motherhood

I have been my happiest and unhappiest.

I have felt both utterly useless and incredibly powerful.

It has been soul-giving and trench-living.

It has uncovered my triggers, yet also my purpose.

Sometimes all in one day.

LIFE HACKS FOR MUMS

A selection put together by thousands of mums

Wash/cut veggies and put them in the fridge for fast snacks and easy meal prep.

Use a slow cooker to organise dinner early in the day.

Get your kids in the bath then into their pyjamas straight after day-care/school as it means there'll be less washing to do, rids them of school germs and saves time after dinner.

Use a shower curtain under the highchair for easy clean up.

To keep them still, give your toddler a 'no' item to investigate during nappy change.

Check the weather forecast for the week then lay out a week's worth of outfits, each with a nappy already in them.

For some noisy entertainment, let your children explore the pots and pans cupboard with a wooden spoon while you cook dinner.

Attach bubble mixture containers to the legs of outdoor furniture with tape to stop spills.

Water changes everything especially your child's mood – whether it's a river, sea, sprinkler, shower, bath, hose or bucket.

Before giving your children sheets of stickers, peel the surrounds off first. This makes it easier for children to peel the stickers off.

Let kids do more things. Even if it means it's slower and a bigger mess, they learn faster.

Flip dinner and lunch meals – cook a big meal for lunch and a smaller one for dinner.

Put a large tub in the car boot to throw nappies, sunscreen and wipes in.

Put sheets inside their matching pillow cases. This makes it much easier to find a set in the linen cupboard.

Make lunchboxes up even in the holidays. This will save constant snacking and asking for food.

Put baby in the front pack while hanging out the washing or doing grocery shopping.

Use zip-up sleepsuits for babies from 0-3 months as it'll mean you have no poppers to line up in the middle of the night.

Layer your crib with a mattress protector/ sheet three times. Take off one layer as needed. Fully made bed instantly.

Put baby in the washing basket while you cook dinner.

Put the kids to bed in the next day's clothes.

Read a bedtime story to the kids in the bath so they can go straight to bed afterwards.

Prepare the kids' lunches the night before.

Make a list of everyone's birthdays at the start of the year and buy all of their birthday cards in January.

Write out a weekly menu for dinners at the start of the week.

When kids are older, give them a basket each for their washing. Put their clean washing in their basket for them to fold and put away themselves.

Always keep an emergency bag in the boot of the car – include nappies, baby wipes, a change of clothes (for baby and mum) and snacks.

Make kids a platter they can snack on in between meals.

Put baby in an empty bath or Portacot with toys.

If possible, get your groceries delivered.

Hang wet washing on coat hangers on the line.

Feed children dinner in the bath if home late.

Make up beds with two complete sets, easy to change sheets.

Got a heap of washing? Go to the laundromat.

When cooking dinner, make extra so you have leftovers for lunch the next day.

Have a toy rotation system – less toys out means less mess to clean up.

Have a basket to fill during clean up. Way easier to put away around the house.

Before wrapping birthday or Christmas presents, take the toys out of their packaging as it makes it way easier to clean up.

If you're not keen on a restaurant's kids' menu, buy side dishes for your children instead.

Fold the washing as soon as you bring it in from the line.

Shave your legs over a bowl of water while the kids do water play next to you.

Heartfelt thanks

To the women of The Motherhood Project community.

To my mum and dad, Suzanne and Brent, for your unwavering dedication
and love all my life.

To my in-laws, Sharon and Max and Pip and Bronya, for your support
and adoration of our children.

To my go to's – Bridge, Nic, Matt and Ro.

To Mary, Rose, Annie, Alice, Rachel, Lauren, Jen and my other treasured friends
who have shared the highs and lows of early motherhood with me.

To Wilding Books – Bex, Craig and Laura – for making dreams come true.